D1281217

My First

1000

Words in

FRENCH

This book belongs to:

....

....

Illustrated by Jan Lewis

English language consultant: Betty Root
French language consultant: Kate Naylor

This is a Parragon Publishing book
First published in 2004

Parragon Publishing
Queen Street House
4 Queen Street
Bath BA1 1HE, UK

Copyright © Parragon 2004
All rights reserved. No part of this publication may be reproduced, stored in a
retrieval system, or transmitted by any means, mechanical, photocopying,
recording or otherwise, without the prior permission of the copyright holder.

ISBN 1-40543-212-8

Printed in India

Contents

About this book

My First 1000 Words in French is the perfect introduction to learning French. In this book you will find over 1000 French words, each with its own picture. The large, central pictures of everyday scenes include all the pictures in the surrounding border. It's fun to find objects in the big pictures and see if you can remember their French name.

At the back of the book you will find four pages of useful phrases in French. On these pages you can find out how to say hello to people in French, how to ask a person's name or age, how to say what you do and don't like, how to talk about your favorite hobbies, and so on.

You will also find an English–French word list that lists, in alphabetical order, all the words illustrated in this book. For each English word you will find its French translation, as well as an easy-to-read pronunciation.

Learning French

About le, la, l', and les

- Every noun in French begins with the word **le**, **la**, **l'**, or **les**, which means "the."
- Words that begin with **le** are masculine—for example **le lapin**, which means "rabbit."
- Words that begin with **la** are feminine—for example **la porte**, which means "door."
- Words that begin with **a**, **e**, **i**, **o**, or **u** (and some words that begin with **h**) have **l'** in front of them—for example **l'argent**, which means "money," and **l'homme**, which means "man."
- Words in the plural have **les** in front—for example **les légumes**, which means "vegetables."
- All French nouns should be learned with their correct "the" word.

About pronunciation

- In French many letters are pronounced in a different way from the way we say them in English. The best way of learning to speak French is to listen to French people when they talk, and to try and copy the way they say words. Here are some general hints about pronouncing French:

- The letters **an** and **on** are pronounced like the "on" of the English word "gong"—for example, **grand** (big) and **bonjour** (hello).

- When it appears before an "e" or an "i," the letter **c** is pronounced like the "s" of the English word "seat"—for example **merci** (thank you); when it appears before other letters, the letter **c** is pronounced like the "c" of the English word "car"—for example **le camion** (truck).

- The letters **ch** are pronounced like the "sh" of the English word "shampoo"—for example **le chat** (cat).

- The letters **eu** are pronounced like the "ur" of the English word "hurt"—for example **neuf** (new) and **bleu** (blue).

- You do not pronounce the letter **h**—for example **l'hôpital** (hospital).

- The letter **j** is pronounced like the "g" of the English word "giant"—for example **jeune** (young) and **le journal** (newspaper).

- The letters **th** are pronounced like the "t" of the English word "tent"—for example **le thé** (tea).

- The letter **u** is pronounced like the "ew" of the English word "few"—for example **le musée** (museum) and **le numéro** (number).

About accents

- In some French words you will see a special mark, called an accent, over certain letters. There are several different kinds of accent. Accents usually appear over the letters e, a, i, and o.

- An accent changes the way that you say a word. Here are some examples of French words with accents:
  l'école (school)   **la tête** (head)
  le frère (brother)   **le sac à main** (purse)

 les doigts de pied

 la main

 le genou

 le coude

 le ventre

 l'épaule

 l'ongle

 les hanches

 la cheville

 le torse

 la taille

 le bras

 le dos

 le pouce

 la jambe

 le doigt

 le pied

 le derrière

 le talon

la tête

l'oreille

l'oeil

les dents

le front

la langue

la bouche

le nez

le cou

les cheveux

le menton

la joue

Ma famille

le père

la soeur

le frère

la mère

la grand-mère

le grand-père

la cousine

l'oncle

la tante

le fauteuil

le vase

l'étagère

le CD

la télévision

le tableau

le parapluie

le miroir

la chaîne stéréo

la chaise berçante

la porte

le téléphone

la clé

la radio

la lampe

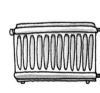
le radiateur

les livres

l'ampoule

les fleurs

le sofa

À la maison

le placard

l'horloge

le luminaire

le tapis

le journal

le magnétoscope

l'interrupteur

la photo

la fenêtre

le bibelot

le coussin

le tabouret

la poignée
de porte

la bibliothèque

le cellulaire

la moquette

le bougeoir

les rideaux

les magazines

9

Les vêtements

le pantalon

la chemise

le chapeau

le T-shirt

la ceinture

les gants

la veste

le caleçon

le tricot

le jean

le gilet

les chaussures

l'imperméable

la jupe

les chaussettes

la casquette

les sandales

la robe

le chandail

le gilet de costume

l'écharpe

le collant

le manteau

les baskets

le short

le maillot de bain

10

L'alimentation

le petit déjeuner

le déjeuner

le dîner

le sel

le poivre

le hamburger

le pain grillé

les biscuits

la laitue

la salade

la limonade

les crêpes

la céréale

le steak

le jambon

la marmelade

le pain

le miel

le café

le thé

les frites

la soupe

le sucre

les pois

les spaghettis

11

la soucoupe

la planche
à repasser

le batteur

la pelle

le balai

le fer
à repasser

le pichet

le tablier

la machine à laver

la table

la casserole

le tabouret

le lave-vaisselle

le verre

le couteau

la mitaine
à four

la cuisinière

la chaise

la fourchette

À la cuisine

le grille-pain

l'essuie-tout

le calendrier

l'évier

la tasse

la cuiller

le coquetier

l'assiette

la chaise haute

la théière

la grande tasse

la bouilloire

le réfrigérateur

la brosse

la poêle à frire

l'aspirateur

la balance

le chiffon

la prise de courant

le rouleau à pâtisserie

la remise

le papillon

la coccinelle

le tuyau
d'arrosage

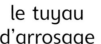
le ver
de terre

la tondeuse à gazon

le chemin

la mangeoire

le buisson

la pelle

la fourche

le nid

le râteau

la binette

l'arbre

l'arrosoir

les feuilles

l'escargot

l'abeille

l'herbe

la guêpe

la corde à linge

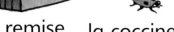

les graines

la balançoire

le chien

le hamac

la laisse

le transplantoir

Au jardin

la haie

le toit

le feu

la serre

la fumée

le pigeon

l'arroseur

l'os

la brouette

la chenille

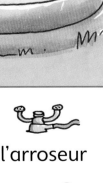
la niche

les noisettes

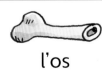
la pataugeuse

le barbecue

la voiture

la bicyclette

la poubelle

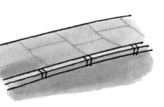
le magasin

le cône

l'échelle

le parcmètre

le trottoir

l'homme

l'ambulance

le marteau-piqueur

l'étal

le banc

le facteur

le café

la boîte à ordures

la pompe à essence

le sac à commissions

le camion

la camionnette

le lampadaire

le policier

l'autobus

la moto

la station-service

la femme

les ordures

le pompier

l'arrêt
d'autobus

le taxi

les marches

les tuyaux

la voiture de police

la poussette

l'égout

la pelleteuse

la cabine
téléphonique

le camion de pompiers

le chariot

la confiture

le lait

les boîtes de
conserve

la poire

les poivrons

le ketchup

les champignons

le beurre

le sac à main

le riz

les oranges

le reçu

les pommes

les saucisses

l'épi de maïs

le jus de fruit

les légumes

les oeufs

la banane

les pommes
de terre

18

les carottes

le fromage

la prune

les tomates

les bouteilles

la carte de crédit

le panier

la liste

les fraises

les cerises

l'oignon

la pastèque

l'ananas

le porte-monnaie

la caisse

le poulet

les pâtes

la viande

l'argent

le concombre

les citrons

les raisins

la baguette
magique

l'ours
en peluche

le tricycle

le voilier

les patins
à roulette

le hochet

la batte

la guitare

la poupée

les briques

le masque

la voiture
de course

la maison
de poupées

la corde à sauter

le fort

le tambour

les quilles

les dés

le diable à ressort

le cheval
à bascule

la marionnette

la flèche

les billes

Au magasin de jouets

la boîte à
peinture

la fusée

le casse-tête

la boîte à outils

l'astronaute

le ballon

la boîte

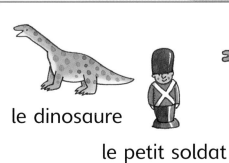
le dinosaure

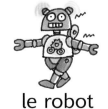
le petit soldat

le robot

le casque

l'arc

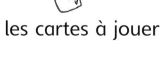
les cartes à jouer

la patinette

l'alphabet

la corbeille
à papier

la colle

l'ordinateur

les feutres

l'imprimante

l'aquarium

les ciseaux

le tableau noir

le xylophone

le cahier

la boîte
à lunch

l'affiche

la souris

le piano

les crayons
de couleur

la flûte

le pinceau

le hamster

la cage

la peinture

À l'école

le chevalet

le violon

le pot
de peinture

le tableau

la maîtresse

la mappemonde

la carte

la règle

la pince
à linge

le bureau

le papier

le clavier

la pâte
à modeler

le poisson

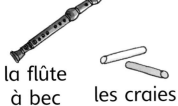
la flûte
à bec

les craies

les plantes

les punaises

le crayon

la gomme
à effacer

la trompette

23

le canoë

le deltaplane

le jogging

le saut en hauteur

le squash

le surf

la voile

le saut en longueur

la natation

les haltères

le hockey

le ski nautique

le plongeon

la boxe

l'équitation

le hockey sur glace

le football

le football américain

le tennis

la planche à neige

l'aviron

le rugby

le basket-ball

le baseball

le patin à glace

la gymnastique

le karting

le tennis de table

la planche à voile

le badminton

le tir à l'arc

le cricket

le karaté

le netball

la bicyclette

le ski

la corde

le bac à sable

le protège-coude

la sucette

les oiseaux

le manège

la rame

les sandwichs

le panneau d'informations

la glissoire

la brindille

la fontaine

la table de pique-nique

la plate-bande

la fille   la genouillère

le bassin

le cadre suédois

 les enfants

la grenouille

 le cerf-volant

la libellule

les têtards

 la branche

 le marchand de glaces

 la barque

 le garçon

 le gardien de parc

 les canetons

 le lapin

 la bascule

 la barrière

 le skateboard

 le bocal

 la crème glacée

 le cygne

 le pique-nique

le chapeau
d'anniversaire

les croustilles

le ruban
adhésif

la paille

la carte
d'anniversaire

le noeud
papillon

la salade
de fruits

le cow-boy

les peintures
de maquillage

la cape

le maïs
éclaté

la sirène

le film

le cadeau

la chaîne
de papier

le bonbon

la robe
d'anniversaire

le sac
de fête

les bougies

le caméscope

La fête d'anniversaire

l'appareil photo

le ballon

le pirate

le collier

le gâteau

la boîte d'allumettes

le magicien

les petits pains

le ruban

le gobelet en papier

la serviette

le chocolat

la nappe

le papier cadeau

la banderole

la cassette

l'allumette

la pizza

le chapeau haut de forme

29

le patient

le plâtre

la canne

le mobile

le fauteuil roulant

le moniteur

la bande dessinée

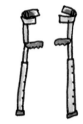
les béquilles

le bandage

les jouets

le plateau

le sang

l'infirmier

le casque

la coupe
de fruits

la radio

la pince à épiler

la couverture

la trousse
d'urgence

le déambulateur

le thermomètre

l'ascenseur

l'écharpe

le docteur

l'enveloppe

le pansement

le brancardier

les mouchoirs en papier

le stéthoscope

les pantoufles

la montre

le médicament

la robe de chambre

la blouse

l'oreiller

les cachets

la civière

le drap

l'ambulancier

le coton

le steward

la tour de contrôle

la pile

la valise

le porte-bagages

l'étiquette

le coffre

la billetterie

les phares

l'avion

les billets

le kiosque

la contrôleuse

le quai

la ville

le sifflet

les rails

le capot

l'aéroport

le conducteur

le gros porteur

le passeport

la mallette

la dépanneuse

l'hélicoptère

la montgolfière

l'aile

le sac à dos

la gare

le dirigeable

la roue

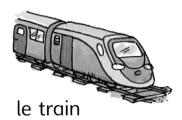
le train

le drapeau

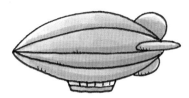
l'escalier roulant

les montagnes russes

le labyrinthe

le jeu d'ordinateur

la barbe à papa

les autos tamponneuses

le hot-dog

le cierge magique

le cirque

la grande roue

les beignets

le tapis

le radeau

le toboggan

le restaurant

le feu d'artifice

l'équilibriste

le château

l'acrobate

le château gonflable

Monsieur Loyal

le manège

le toboggan

la piscine

le train fantôme

le cinéma

le clown

le déguisement

le plongeoir

le trampoline

les bulles

le jeu de quilles

la fanfare

le musée

la jongleuse

le pêcheur

le renard

le feu de camp

le rocher

le sac de couchage

la tente

les mûres

la remorque

la chute d'eau

le crapaud

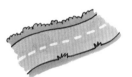
la route

le héron

la colline

l'église

l'écluse

le cheval

le bûcheron

le nuage

le ciel

le lac

le tunnel

le lièvre

le moulin

le moulin

la rivière

les bûches

la canne à pêche

le fil barbelé

la hache

la chouette

le papillon
de nuit

le pont

la forêt

la caravane

la berge

le canal

la cabane
en rondins

le campeur

la montagne

le veau

 le tonneau

 la moissonneuse-batteuse

 l'âne

 les canards

l'agneau

 le champ

 le mouton

 la chèvre

 la poule

 le chien de berger

 la porcherie

 le tracteur

 la terre

 le fermier

 les chatons

les bottes

la grange

la charrue

la dinde

 le camion-citerne

le chevreau

la maison
de ferme

le sac

le poulain

l'épouvantail

les poussins

l'abreuvoir

 À la ferme

le verger

le taureau

le mur

le cochon

la selle

les petits
cochons

la vache

l'écurie

le blé

le chat

la paille

le seau

le coq

le poulailler

l'oie

le foin

39

le château de sable

les brassards

le canot

le sable

le ferry

les coquillages

la bouée

la vague

le canoë

l'île

les palmes

la corde

la méduse

les galets

l'épuisette

le maître nageur

la voile

la combinaison

la falaise

la bouteille thermos

les lunettes
de soleil

l'étoile
de mer

l'algue

le bikini

la barque à moteur

l'ancre

la crème
solaire

la sucette
glacée

la mouette

le crabe

le chapeau
de soleil

la bouée

la chaîne

la planche de surf

le ballon de plage

le phare

la mer

la crevette

les lunettes de plongée

la mare

la chaise
longue

le tube

le parasol

La chambre

le lit

la suce

l'armoire

le pyjama

le peigne

la bouillotte

le crochet

le bébé

la brosse
à cheveux

le réveil

la couette

la nuit

le berceau

le cintre

la chemise de nuit

le store

la commode

le lit de bébé

la boîte à jouets

les lits superposés

42

le shampooing

la baignoire

l'eau

les toilettes

la serviette

la brosse à dents

le robinet

le savon

le bouchon

le dentifrice

le papier
de toilette

l'éponge

la couche

le gant de toilette

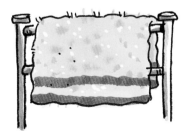
le porte-serviettes

le lavabo

le bain moussant

la douche

 couper

 brosser

 laver

 regarder

 attraper

 souffler

 pleurer

 lécher

 pourchasser

 lire

 grimper

 creuser

 acheter

 dormir

 sauter

 écouter

 applaudir

 faire la queue

 écrire

 tirer

 pousser

 embrasser

 danser

nager

cueillir

jouer

faire du vélo

tricoter

cuisiner

plonger

rire

sauter à la corde

sourire

marcher

porter

boire

courir

s'asseoir

se tenir debout

manger

ramer

chanter

dedans

 dehors

 bas

 haut

 heureux

 triste

 en dessous

 au-dessus

 froid

 chaud

 mouillé

 sec

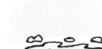 dur

 doux

 mince

 gros

 vide

 plein

 propre

 sale

 sombre

 clair

46

long

court

dessus

vieux

neuf

dessous

près

loin

haut

petit

grand

lent

rapide

bas

peu

nombreux

ouvert

fermé

 le dentiste

 l'acteur

 le cuisinier

 la jardinière

 le danseur

 la serveuse

 la scientifique

la chanteuse

 le décorateur

 l'artiste

 le coiffeur

 le plombier

 le maçon

 la secrétaire

 la fleuriste

 le juge

 l'éboueur

 le boucher

 l'électricien

 le plongeur

le réceptionniste

Les gens

le marin

le sorcier

la sorcière

le laveur de carreaux

la musicienne

le patineur

le charpentier

la présentatrice

le boulanger

le chauffeur d'autobus

la journaliste

la bibliothécaire

le mécanicien

le pilote

le serveur

la potière

le grimpeur

le camionneur

l'apiculteur

49

l'éléphant

le singe

les lionceaux

la girafe

le zèbre

le cerf

le guépard

la tortue

le gorille

le rhinocéros

le castor

le chameau

la baleine

l'ours

le lézard

le flamant rose

le loup

l'autruche

le kangourou

l'ours polaire

le chimpanzé

le toucan

le requin

le lion

le léopard

le paon

le pingouin

le perroquet

le crocodile

le serpent

l'otarie

l'aigle

le dauphin

le raton laveur

le koala

le tigre

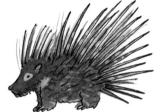

le porc-épic

le renne

le macareux

l'hippopotame

l'alligator

le pélican

le panda

Les numéros

un	🐞	20	vingt
deux	🐤🐤	30	trente
trois	🧁🧁🧁	40	quarante
quatre	🪣🪣🪣🪣	50	cinquante
cinq	🏐🏐🏐🏐🏐	60	soixante
six	🎈🎈🎈🎈🎈🎈	70	soixante-dix
sept	⭐⭐⭐⭐⭐⭐⭐	80	quatre-vingts
huit	🧦🧦🧦🧦🧦🧦🧦🧦	90	quatre-vingt-dix
neuf	🚩🚩🚩🚩🚩🚩🚩🚩🚩	100	cent
dix	🐱🐱🐱🐱🐱🐱🐱🐱🐱🐱		
onze			
douze			
treize			
quatorze			
quinze			
seize			
dix-sept			
dix-huit			
dix-neuf			
vingt			

Les couleurs

violet

jaune

noir

rouge

orange

bleu

gris

vert

blanc

brun

rose

Les formes

le croissant

le cercle

le triangle

le losange

l'étoile

le rectangle

le carré

l'ovale

l'octogone

l'hexagone

53

Les jours de la semaine

lundi

mardi

mercredi

jeudi

vendredi

samedi

dimanche

Les mois de l'année

janvier

février

mars

avril

mai

juin

juillet

août

septembre

octobre

novembre

décembre

Le temps

la pluie

le soleil

la neige

le vent

l'arc-en-ciel

l'éclair

le gel

le brouillard

Les saisons

le printemps

l'été

l'automne

l'hiver

54

Useful phrases and English–French word list

Useful phrases

Greeting people

bonjour	hello
salut	hi
bonsoir	good evening
bonne nuit	goodnight
au revoir	goodbye
Monsieur	Sir or Mr.
Madame	Madam or Mrs.
Mademoiselle	Miss

Being polite

s'il vous plaît	please
merci	thank you
merci beaucoup	thank you very much
oui	yes
non	no
merci, monsieur	thank you (talking to a man)
oui, madame	yes (talking to a woman)
pardon	excuse me

Making friends

comment t'appelles-tu?	what is your name?
je m'appelle ...	my name is ...
où habites-tu?	where do you live?
j'habite ...	I live ...
quel âge as-tu?	how old are you?
j'ai (neuf) ans.	I am (nine) years old.

Introducing people

voici	here is
il s'appelle	his name is
elle s'appelle	her name is
mon	my (for **le** words—**mon frère**)
ma	my (for **la** words—**ma soeur**)
voici ma soeur	here is my sister
mon frère s'appelle ...	my brother is called

Asking about things

qu'est-ce que c'est?	what is it?
c'est ...	it is ...
un	a (for **le** words—**un lit**)
une	a (for **la** words—**une serviette**)
c'est un lit	it is a bed
où est ...?	where is ...?
où sont ...?	where are ...?
dans	in
derrière	behind
sur	on
sous	under
la télévision est sur la table	the television is on the table
les magazines sont sous la table	the magazines are under the table

Saying what you like and don't like

j'aime	I like
j'aime bien	I like a lot
j'adore	I love
je n'aime pas	I don't like
je n'aime pas tellement	I don't really like
je déteste	I hate
aimes-tu ...?	do you like ...?
j'aime le chocolat.	I like chocolate.
j'adore danser.	I love dancing.

Asking for things

avez-vous ...?	do you have ...?
je voudrais ...	I would like ...
c'est combien?	how much is it?
est-ce qu'il y a ...?	is there ...?
il y a ...	there is ...
voilà!	there you are!

Saying what you have and don't have

j'ai	I have
j'ai un chien	I have a dog
je n'ai pas	I don't have
il a	he has
elle a	she has
as-tu?	do you have?

Talking about your hobbies

je joue	I play
je joue au tennis	I play tennis
je fais	I do
je ne joue pas	I don't play
je ne fais pas	I don't do
j'aime jouer	I like playing
je n'aime pas faire	I don't like doing
que fais-tu?	what are you doing?

Being ill

je suis malade	I'm ill
j'ai mal à la tête	I've got a headache
j'ai mal à l'oreille	I've got earache

Talking about what people and things are like

comment c'est?	what is it like?
c'est	it is
c'est grand	it's big
c'est petit	it's small
je suis	I am
il est	he is
elle est	she is
il est heureux	he is happy
elle est triste	she is sad

Talking about what people do

mon père est artiste	my father is an artist
ma mère est dentiste	my mother is a dentist
je voudrais être ...	I would like to be ...

Other useful doing words

je vais	I'm going
je porte	I'm wearing
je mange	I'm eating
je bois	I'm drinking

English–French word list

a

above	**dessus**	[dessu]
acrobat	**l'acrobate** (m/f)	[akrobat]
actor	**l'acteur** (m)	[akter]
adhesive tape	**le ruban adhésif**	[rubaun-adezif]
airplane	**l'avion** (m)	[aveeon]
airport	**l'aéroport** (m)	[aero-por]
airship	**le dirigeable**	[dee-ree-jabl]
air steward	**le steward**	[steeoowart]
alarm clock	**le réveil**	[revay]
alligator	**l'alligator** (m)	[alligator]
alphabet	**l'alphabet** (m)	[alfabeh]
ambulance	**l'ambulance** (f)	[aumbulauns]
anchor	**l'ancre** (f)	[aunkr]
animal	**l'animal** (m)	[aneemal]
ankle	**la cheville**	[sheveeye]
apple	**la pomme**	[pom]
April	**avril**	[avreel]
apron	**le tablier**	[tahblee-eh]
archery	**le tir à l'arc**	[teer-ah-lark]
arm	**le bras**	[bra]
armband	**le brassard**	[brassar]
armchair	**le fauteuil**	[foteuy]
arrow	**la flèche**	[flesh]
artist	**l'artiste** (m/f)	[arteest]
astronaut	**l'astronaute** (m/f)	[astronoht]
August	**août**	[oot]
aunt	**la tante**	[taunt]
ax	**la hache**	[ash]

b

baby	**le bébé**	[behbeh]
back	**le dos**	[doe]
backpack	**le sac à dos**	[sack-ah-doe]
badminton	**le badminton**	[badminton]
baker	**le boulanger**	[boolaunjeh]
ball	**le ballon**	[balloun]
balloon	**le ballon**	[balloun]
banana	**la banane**	[banan]
band	**la fanfare**	[fanfar]
bandage	**le bandage**	[baundahj]
banner	**la banderole**	[baunderohl]
barbecue	**le barbecue**	[barbekwiu]
barbed wire	**le fil barbelé**	[feel-barbeleh]
barge	**la berge**	[bairj]

barn	**la grange**	[graunj]
barrel	**le tonneau**	[tono]
baseball	**le baseball**	[baseball]
basket	**le panier**	[pahneeyeh]
basketball	**le basket-ball**	[basketball]
bat	**la batte**	[bat]
bathrobe	**la robe de chambre**	[rob-duh-shaumbr]
bathroom	**la salle de bains**	[sal-duh-banh]
bathroom tissue	**le papier de toilette**	[papeeyeh-duh-twalett]
bathtub	**la baignoire**	[baignwar]
battery	**la pile**	[peel]
beach	**la plage**	[plahj]
beach ball	**le ballon de plage**	[balon-duh-plahj]
bear	**l'ours** (m)	[oors]
beaver	**le castor**	[kastor]
bed	**le lit**	[lee]
bedroom	**la chambre**	[shombr]
bee	**l'abeille** (f)	[abbay]
beekeeper	**l'apiculteur** (m)	[apeeculter]
bell pepper	**le poivron**	[pwavrohn]
below	**dessous**	[dessoo]
belt	**la ceinture**	[san-tur]
bicycle	**la bicyclette**	[beeseeklet]
big	**grand**	[graun]
bikini	**le bikini**	[beekeenee]
bird	**l'oiseau** (m)	[wahzoh]
bird table	**la mangeoire**	[maunjwar]
birthday	**l'anniversaire** (m)	[anivairsair]
birthday card	**la carte d'anniversaire**	[kart-danivairsair]
black	**noir**	[nwar]
blackberry	**la mûre**	[mewr]
blanket	**la couverture**	[koovertur]
blind	**le store**	[stor]
blood	**le sang**	[saun]
blow	**souffler**	[soofleh]
blue	**bleu**	[blur]
boat	**la barque**	[bark]
bone	**l'os** (m)	[ohss]
bonfire	**le feu**	[fuh]
book	**le livre**	[leevr]
bookcase	**la bibliothèque**	[bibliotek]
boot	**la botte**	[bott]
booth	**l'étal** (m)	[ehtal]
bottle	**la bouteille**	[booteh-e]
bottom	**le derrière**	[deriair]
bouncy castle	**le château gonflable**	[shato-gon-flabl]

bow	**l'arc** (m)	[ark]
bowling	**le jeu de quilles**	[jeuh-duh-keeye]
bowling pin	**la quille**	[keeye]
bow tie	**le noeud papillon**	[nur-papeeyon]
box	**la boîte**	[bwat]
boxing	**la boxe**	[boks]
boy	**le garçon**	[gahr-sonn]
branch	**la branche**	[branch]
bread	**le pain**	[pan]
bread roll	**le petit pain**	[petee-pan]
breakfast	**le petit déjeuner**	[puhtee-day-juhnay]
brick	**la brique**	[brik]
bricklayer	**le maçon**	[mahsson]
bridge	**le pont**	[ponh]
briefcase	**la mallette**	[mahlett]
broom	**le balai**	[bahleh]
brother	**le frère**	[frair]
brown	**brun**	[brun]
brush (noun)	**la brosse**	[bross]
brush (verb)	**brosser**	[brosseh]
bubble	**la bulle**	[bul]
bubblebath	**le bain moussant**	[banh-moosaun]
bull	**le taureau**	[toroh]
bumper cars	**les autos tamponneuses** (f)	[oto-taum-poneuz]
bunk beds	**les lits superposés** (m)	[lee-superpozeh]
buoy	**la bouée**	[booweh]
burger	**le hamburger**	[haun-bourger]
bus	**l'autobus** (m)	[ohtobewss]
bus driver	**le chauffeur d'autobus**	[shofer-dohtobewss]
bush	**le buisson**	[bwissoun]
bus stop	**l'arrêt d'autobus** (m)	[areh-dohtobewss]
butcher	**le boucher**	[boosheh]
butter	**le beurre**	[burr]
butterfly	**le papillon**	[papeeyon]
buy	**acheter**	[ashteh]

C

cab	**le taxi**	[taksee]
café	**le café**	[kafeh]
cage	**la cage**	[kahj]
cake	**le gâteau**	[gahtoh]
calendar	**le calendrier**	[kalaundrieh]
calf	**le veau**	[voh]
camcorder	**le caméscope**	[kamehscope]
camel	**le chameau**	[shamoh]
camera	**l'appareil photo** (m)	[aparey-foto]
camper	**le campeur**	[kaumper]
campfire	**le feu de camp**	[feu-duh-kaun]
can	**la boîte de conserve**	[bwat-duh-konserv]
canal	**le canal**	[kanal]
candle	**la bougie**	[boohjee]
candlestick	**le bougeoir**	[boojooar]
candy	**le bonbon**	[bounboun]
canoe	**le canoë**	[kanoeh]
canoeing	**le canoë**	[kanoeh]
cap	**la casquette**	[kaskette]
cape	**la cape**	[kap]
car	**la voiture**	[vwa-toor]
cardigan	**le gilet**	[jilai]
carousel	**le manège**	[manej]
carpenter	**le charpentier**	[sharpauntieh]
carpet	**la moquette**	[mockette]
carrot	**la carotte**	[karot]
carry	**porter**	[porteh]
cassette	**la cassette**	[kahset]
castle	**le château**	[shatoh]
cat	**le chat**	[sha]
catch	**attraper**	[atrapeh]
caterpillar	**la chenille**	[sheneeye]
cellphone	**le cellulaire**	[sayloolair]
cereal	**la céréale**	[saireahl]
chain	**la chaîne**	[shen]
chair	**la chaise**	[shez]
chalk	**la craie**	[kreh]
chalkboard	**le tableau noir**	[tahbloh-nwar]
change purse	**le porte-monnaie**	[port-moneh]
chase	**pourchasser**	[poorshasseh]
checkout	**la caisse**	[kess]
cheek	**la joue**	[jooh]
cheese	**le fromage**	[fromahj]
cheetah	**le guépard**	[gehpar]
cherry	**la cerise**	[sereez]
chest	**le torse**	[tors]
chick	**le poussin**	[poosan]
chicken	**le poulet**	[pooleh]
child	**l'enfant** (m/f)	[aunfaun]
chimpanzee	**le chimpanzé**	[shunpaunzeh]
chin	**le menton**	[mauntoun]
chocolate	**le chocolat**	[shokolah]
church	**l'église** (f)	[egleez]

circle	**le cercle**	[serkl]
circus	**le cirque**	[seerk]
clap	**applaudir**	[aplodeer]
clean	**propre**	[propr]
cliff	**la falaise**	[falehz]
climb	**grimper**	[grunpeh]
climber	**le grimpeur**	[grunper]
clock	**l'horloge** (f)	[orloje]
closed	**fermé**	[fermeh]
closet	**le placard**	[plakar]
clothes	**les vêtements**	[vait-maun]
clothesline	**la corde à linge**	[kord-ah-lunj]
clothespin	**la pince à linge**	[punss-ah-lunj]
cloud	**le nuage**	[nuahj]
clown	**le clown**	[kloon]
coat (doctor's)	**la blouse**	[blooz]
coffee	**le café**	[kafeh]
cold	**froid**	[frwa]
color	**la couleur**	[kooler]
coloring pencil	**le crayon de couleur**	[kreyoun-duh-kooleur]
comb	**le peigne**	[paign]
combine harvester	**la moissonneuse-batteuse**	[mwasoneuz-bateuz]
comforter	**la couette**	[kwett]
comic book	**la bande dessinée**	[baund-dessineh]
compact disc	**le CD**	[say-day]
computer	**l'ordinateur** (m)	[ordeenater]
computer game	**le jeu d'ordinateur**	[jeu-dordeenater]
conductor (man)	**le contrôleur**	[kontroler]
conductor (woman)	**la contrôleuse**	[kontrolerz]
control tower	**la tour de contrôle**	[toor-duh-kontroll]
cook (verb)	**cuisiner**	[kwisineh]
cook (noun)	**le cuisinier**	[kwizinieh]
cookie	**le biscuit**	[biskwi]
corn on the cob	**l'épi de maïs** (m)	[epee-duh-maieess]
costume	**le déguisement**	[deguize-maun]
cotton candy	**la barbe à papa**	[barb-ah-papa]
cotton ball	**le coton**	[koton]
couch	**le sofa**	[sofa]
countryside	**la campagne**	[kampagn]
cousin	**la cousine**	[koozine]
cow	**la vache**	[vash]
cowboy	**le cow-boy**	[koboy]
crab	**le crabe**	[krab]
cradle	**le berceau**	[bersoh]
credit card	**la carte de crédit**	[kart-duh-kredee]
crescent	**le croissant**	[krwasaun]
crib	**le lit de bébé**	[lee-duh-bebeh]
cricket	**le cricket**	[kriket]
crocodile	**le crocodile**	[krokodeel]
crutch	**la béquille**	[behkeeye]
cry	**pleurer**	[pleureh]
cucumber	**le concombre**	[konkonbr]
cup	**la tasse**	[tass]
cushion	**le coussin**	[koossun]
cut	**couper**	[koopeh]
cycle	**faire du vélo**	[fair-doo-vehloh]
cycling	**la bicyclette**	[beeseeklet]

d

dance	**danser**	[daunseh]
dancer	**le danseur**	[daunser]
dark	**sombre**	[sombr]
day	**le jour**	[joor]
December	**décembre**	[desaumbr]
deckchair	**la chaise longue**	[shehz-long]
decorator	**le décorateur**	[dekorater]
deer	**le cerf**	[sehr]
dentist	**le/la dentiste**	[daunteest]
desk	**le bureau**	[buroh]
diamond	**le losange**	[lozaunj]
diaper	**la couche**	[koosh]
dice	**les dés** (m)	[deh]
dig	**creuser**	[kreuzeh]
digger	**la pelleteuse**	[pelteuz]
dinghy	**le canot**	[kanoh]
dinner	**le dîner**	[deeneh]
dinosaur	**le dinosaure**	[deenohzor]
dirty	**sale**	[sahl]
dishwasher	**le lave-vaisselle**	[lahv-vehsel]
dive	**plonger**	[plonjeh]
diver	**le plongeur**	[plonjer]
diving	**le plongeon**	[plonjoun]
diving board	**le plongeoir**	[plonjwar]
doctor	**le/la docteur**	[dokteur]
dog	**le chien**	[shee-ann]
doll	**la poupée**	[poopeh]
dolls' house	**la maison de poupées**	[mezoun-duh-poopeh]
dolphin	**le dauphin**	[dofun]

donkey	l'âne (m)	[ahn]
donut	le beignet	[beneeyeh]
door	la porte	[port]
door handle	la poignée de porte	[pwagnay-duh-port]
down	bas	[bah]
dragonfly	la libellule	[leebelul]
drain	l'égout (m)	[egooh]
drape	le rideau	[reedoe]
dress	la robe	[rob]
dresser	la commode	[komod]
drill	le marteau-piqueur	[marto-pickeur]
drink	boire	[bwar]
drum	le tambour	[taumboor]
dry	sec	[sehk]
duck	le canard	[kanar]
duckling	le caneton	[kahneton]
dustbin	la poubelle	[poobel]
duster	le chiffon	[sheefong]
dustpan	la pelle	[pehl]

e

eagle	l'aigle (m)	[ehgl]
ear	l'oreille (f)	[oray]
easel	le chevalet	[shevahleh]
eat	manger	[maunjeh]
egg	l'oeuf (m)	[euf]
egg cup	le coquetier	[koketieh]
eight	huit	[uit]
eighteen	dix-huit	[deezuit]
elbow	le coude	[kood]
elbow pad	le protège-coude	[protej-kood]
electrician	l'électricien (m)	[ehlektreesiun]
elephant	l'éléphant (m)	[elehfaun]
elevator	l'ascenseur (m)	[asaunser]
eleven	onze	[onz]
empty	vide	[veed]
envelope	l'enveloppe (f)	[onvehlop]
eraser	la gomme à effacer	[gom-ah-ehfaseh]
escalator	l'escalier roulant (m)	[eskalieh-roolaun]
eye	l'oeil (m)	[eu-y]

f

face paint	la peinture de maquillage	[puntur-duh-makeeyahj]
fall	l'automne (m)	[otonn]
family	la famille	[fameey]

far	loin	[looun]
farm	la ferme	[fairm]
farmer	le fermier	[fairmeeyeh]
farmhouse	la maison de ferme	[mehzon-duh-fairm]
fast	rapide	[rapeed]
fat	gros	[groh]
father	le père	[pair]
faucet	le robinet	[robeeneh]
February	février	[fehvrieh]
felt tip	le feutre	[feutr]
Ferris wheel	la grande roue	[graund-roo]
ferry	le ferry	[ferry]
few	peu	[peuh]
field	le champ	[shaun]
field hockey	le hockey	[hockey]
fifteen	quinze	[kanz]
film	le film	[film]
finger	le doigt	[dwa]
firefighter	le pompier	[poumpieh]
fire truck	le camion de pompiers	[kameeoun-duh-poumpieh]
firework	le feu d'artifice	[feu-darteefiss]
first-aid box	la trousse d'urgence	[troos-durjauns]
fish	le poisson	[pwasson]
fisherman	le pêcheur	[pehsher]
fishing rod	la canne à pêche	[kan-ah-pesh]
five	cinq	[sank]
flag	le drapeau	[drapoh]
flamingo	le flamant rose	[flamaun-rohz]
flask	la bouteille thermos	[booteh-tehrmoss]
flipper	la palme	[palm]
florist	le/la fleuriste	[fleureest]
flower	la fleur	[fleur]
flower-bed	la plate-bande	[plat-baund]
flute	la flûte	[floot]
foal	le poulain	[poolun]
fog	le brouillard	[brooiyar]
food mixer	le batteur	[bahter]
foods	l'alimentation (f)	[ahlee-mont-asseeyon]
foot	le pied	[pee-eh]
football	le football américain	[football-amerikun]
footstool	le tabouret	[tabooreh]
forehead	le front	[froun]
forest	la forêt	[foreh]
fork (garden)	la fourche	[foorsh]

fork (table)	**la fourchette**	[foorshet]	green	**vert**	[vair]
fort	**le fort**	[for]	greenhouse	**la serre**	[sehr]
fountain	**la fontaine**	[fontehn]	grocery bag	**le sac à**	[sak-ah-
four	**quatre**	[katr]		**commissions**	komiseeoun]
fourteen	**quatorze**	[katorz]	guitar	**la guitare**	[geetarr]
fox	**le renard**	[renar]	gymnastics	**la gymnastique**	[gymnastik]
French fries	**les frites** (f)	[freet]			
Friday	**vendredi**	[vaundredee]			
fridge	**le réfrigérateur**	[rehfridgeh-			
		rater]			

h

frog	**la grenouille**	[grenooy]	hair	**les cheveux** (m)	[sherver]
frost	**le gel**	[jehl]	hairbrush	**la brosse**	[bros-ah-
fruit bowl	**la coupe**	[koop-		**à cheveux**	sherver]
	de fruits	duh-frwi]	hairdresser	**le coiffeur**	[kwafer]
fruit juice	**le jus de fruit**	[ju-duh-frwi]	ham	**le jambon**	[jaumbong]
fruit salad	**la salade**	[salad-	hammock	**le hamac**	[amak]
	de fruits	duh-frwi]	hamster	**le hamster**	[amstair]
frying pan	**la poêle à frire**	[pwal-ah-	hand	**la main**	[munh]
		freer]	hanger	**le cintre**	[suntr]
full	**plein**	[plunh]	hang-gliding	**le deltaplane**	[deltaplahn]
			happy	**heureux**	[heuhreuh]

g

			hard	**dur**	[dur]
			hare	**le lièvre**	[lee-aivr]
garbage	**les ordures** (f)	[ordewr]	hat	**le chapeau**	[shapoh]
garbage man	**l'éboueur** (m)	[ebooer]	hay	**le foin**	[fooun]
gardener (man)	**le jardinier**	[jardeeniyeh]	head	**la tête**	[tet]
gardener (woman)	**la jardinière**	[jardeeniair]	headlight	**le phare**	[far]
gas pump	**la pompe**	[poump-	headphones	**le casque**	[kask]
	à essence	ah-esauns]	hedge	**la haie**	[eh]
gas station	**la station-**	[stasyoun-	heel	**le talon**	[tahlong]
	service	sehrviss]	helicopter	**l'hélicoptère** (m)	[elikoptair]
gate	**la barrière**	[bahree-ayr]	helmet	**le casque**	[kask]
ghost train	**le train**	[trun-	hen	**la poule**	[pool]
	fantôme	fauntohm]	henhouse	**le poulailler**	[poolayeh]
gift	**le cadeau**	[kahdo]	heron	**le héron**	[eronh]
giraffe	**la girafe**	[jeeraff]	hexagon	**l'hexagone** (m)	[hegzagohn]
girl	**la fille**	[fee-yuh]	hi-fi	**la chaîne stéréo**	[shen-stereo]
glass	**le verre**	[vair]	high	**haut**	[oh]
globe	**la mappemonde**	[map-mond]	highchair	**la chaise haute**	[shez-oht]
glove	**le gant**	[gaun]	high jump	**le saut**	[soh-
glue	**la colle**	[koll]		**en hauteur**	aun-ohteur]
goat	**la chèvre**	[shevr]	hill	**la colline**	[koleen]
go-cart racing	**le karting**	[karting]	hip	**la hanche**	[haunsh]
goggles	**les lunettes**	[loonet-duh	hippopotamus	**l'hippopotame** (m)	[ipopotam]
	de plongée (f)	plonjay]	hoe	**la binette**	[beenet]
goose	**l'oie** (f)	[wa]	honey	**le miel**	[mee-ehl]
gorilla	**le gorille**	[goreeye]	hood (car)	**le capot**	[kapoh]
grandfather	**le grand-père**	[graun-pair]	hook	**le crochet**	[krosheh]
grandmother	**la grand-mère**	[graun-mair]	horse	**le cheval**	[sheval]
grape	**le raisin**	[rezun]	hose	**le tuyau**	[tuyo-
grass	**l'herbe** (f)	[ehrb]		**d'arrosage**	darozaj]
gray	**gris**	[gree]	hospital	**l'hôpital** (m)	[opeetal]
			hot	**chaud**	[shoh]

hot-air balloon	**la montgolfière**	[mongolf-eeair]
hot dog	**le hot-dog**	[hot-dog]
hot-water bottle	**la bouillotte**	[booyott]
house	**la maison**	[mai-zon]

i

ice cream	**la crème glacée**	[krem-glahseh]
ice-cream truck	**le marchand de glaces**	[marshaun-duh-glass]
ice hockey	**le hockey sur glace**	[hockey-seur-glass]
ice skater	**le patineur**	[pateener]
ice skating	**le patin à glace**	[patun-ah-glass]
in	**dedans**	[dedaun]
iron	**le fer à repasser**	[fair-ah-repasseh]
ironing board	**la planche à repasser**	[plaunsh-ah-repasseh]
island	**l'île** (f)	[eel]

j

jacket	**la veste**	[vest]
jack-in-the-box	**le diable à ressort**	[diahbl-ah-ressohr]
January	**janvier**	[jaunvieh]
jar	**le pot**	[poh]
jeans	**le jean**	[jean]
jelly	**la confiture**	[kounfeetur]
jellyfish	**la méduse**	[mehdooz]
jigsaw puzzle	**le casse-tête**	[kas-tet]
jogging	**le jogging**	[jogging]
journalist	**le/la journaliste**	[joornaleest]
judge	**le juge**	[jooj]
juggler (man)	**le jongleur**	[jongler]
juggler (woman)	**la jongleuse**	[jongleuz]
July	**juillet**	[juiyeh]
jumbo jet	**le gros porteur**	[groh-porter]
jump	**sauter**	[sohteh]
jump rope	**la corde à sauter**	[kord-ah-sohteh]
jungle gym	**le cadre suédois**	[kahdr-su-aydwa]
June	**juin**	[ju-unh]

k

kangaroo	**le kangourou**	[kaungooroo]
karate	**le karaté**	[karateh]
kennel	**la niche**	[neesh]
ketchup	**le ketchup**	[ketchup]
kettle	**la bouilloire**	[boohywar]
key	**la clé**	[kleh]
keyboard	**le clavier**	[klavieh]
kid	**le chevreau**	[shevroh]
kiosk	**le kiosque**	[kiosk]
kiss	**embrasser**	[aumbraseh]
kitchen	**la cuisine**	[kwizine]
kite	**le cerf-volant**	[ser-volaun]
kitten	**le chaton**	[shaton]
knee	**le genou**	[jenooh]
knee pad	**la genouillère**	[jenooyair]
knife	**le couteau**	[kootoh]
knit	**tricoter**	[trikoteh]
koala	**le koala**	[koala]

l

label	**l'étiquette** (f)	[etiket]
ladder	**l'échelle** (f)	[eshel]
ladybug	**la coccinelle**	[koksinel]
lake	**le lac**	[lack]
lamb	**l'agneau** (m)	[agnoh]
lamp	**la lampe**	[laump]
lamp post	**le lampadaire**	[laumpadair]
laugh	**rire**	[reer]
lawnmower	**la tondeuse à gazon**	[toundeuz-ah-gahzoun]
lead	**la laisse**	[less]
leaf	**la feuille**	[feu-y]
leg	**la jambe**	[jaumb]
lemon	**le citron**	[seetroun]
lemonade	**la limonade**	[leemonahde]
leopard	**le léopard**	[lehopar]
lettuce	**la laitue**	[laitew]
librarian	**le/la bibliothécaire**	[beebleeo-tekair]
lick	**lécher**	[lehsheh]
lifeguard	**le maître nageur**	[mehtr-nahjer]
lifesaver	**la bouée**	[buweh]
light (noun)	**le luminaire**	[loominair]
light (adjective)	**clair**	[klair]
light bulb	**l'ampoule** (f)	[aumpool]
lighthouse	**le phare**	[far]
lightning	**l'éclair** (m)	[ehklair]
lion	**le lion**	[leeon]
lion cub	**le lionceau**	[leeonsoh]
list	**la liste**	[leest]
listen	**écouter**	[ekooteh]
lizard	**le lézard**	[lezahr]
lock	**l'écluse** (f)	[ekluz]
log	**la bûche**	[boosh]

log cabin	**la cabane en rondins**	[kaban-aun-rondun]
long	**long**	[lonh]
long jump	**le saut en longueur**	[soh-aun-longeur]
look	**regarder**	[regardeh]
low	**bas**	[bah]
luggage rack	**le porte-bagages**	[port-bagaj]
lunch	**le déjeuner**	[dayjuhnay]
lunch box	**la boîte à lunch**	[bwat-ah-lunch]

m

magazine	**le magazine**	[magazine]
magician	**le magicien**	[majeesiun]
magic wand	**la baguette magique**	[baget-majik]
mailman	**le facteur**	[fakter]
man	**l'homme** (m)	[om]
many	**nombreux**	[nombreu]
map	**la carte**	[kart]
marble	**la bille**	[beeye]
March	**mars**	[mahrss]
marmalade	**la marmelade**	[mahrme-lahde]
mask	**le masque**	[mahsk]
mat	**le tapis**	[tahpee]
match	**l'allumette** (f)	[aloomett]
matchbox	**la boîte d'allumettes**	[bwat-dalumett]
May	**mai**	[meh]
maze	**le labyrinthe**	[labeerunt]
meat	**la viande**	[veeaund]
mechanic	**le mécanicien**	[mekanee-siunh]
medicine	**le médicament**	[medi-kamaun]
mermaid	**la sirène**	[seeren]
merry-go-round	**le manège**	[manehj]
milk	**le lait**	[leh]
mirror	**le miroir**	[meerwar]
mobile	**le mobile**	[mobeel]
modeling clay	**la pâte à modeler**	[paht-ah-modeleh]
Monday	**lundi**	[lundee]
money	**l'argent** (m)	[arjaun]
monitor	**le moniteur**	[moneeteur]
monkey	**le singe**	[sunj]
month	**le mois**	[mwa]
moth	**le papillon de nuit**	[papeeyon-duh-nwee]

mother	**la mère**	[mair]
motorboat	**la barque à moteur**	[bark-ah-mohter]
motorcycle	**la moto**	[moto]
mountain	**la montagne**	[montahgn]
mouse	**la souris**	[sooree]
mouth	**la bouche**	[boosh]
movie theater	**le cinéma**	[sinema]
mug	**la grande tasse**	[graund-tass]
museum	**le musée**	[mewzay]
mushroom	**le champignon**	[shaum-peegnon]
musician (man)	**le musicien**	[muzeesiunh]
musician (woman)	**la musicienne**	[muzeesienn]

n

nail	**l'ongle** (m)	[oungle]
napkin	**la serviette**	[serviet]
near	**près**	[preh]
neck	**le cou**	[koo]
necklace	**le collier**	[koleeyeh]
nest	**le nid**	[nee]
net	**l'épuisette** (f)	[epueezett]
netball	**le netball**	[netball]
new	**neuf**	[neuhf]
newspaper	**le journal**	[joornal]
night	**la nuit**	[nwee]
nightdress	**la chemise de nuit**	[shemeez-duh-nwee]
nine	**neuf**	[neuhf]
nineteen	**dix-neuf**	[deez-neuhf]
nose	**le nez**	[nay]
notice board	**le panneau d'informations**	[pahno-dan-formaseeon]
November	**novembre**	[novaumbr]
number	**le numéro**	[numehroh]
nurse (man)	**l'infirmier**	[anfirmieh]
nurse (woman)	**l'infirmière**	[anfirmierr]
nut	**la noisette**	[nwazet]

o

oar	**la rame**	[ram]
octagon	**l'octogone** (m)	[oktogohn]
October	**octobre**	[oktobr]
old	**vieux**	[vieu]
one	**un**	[uhn]
onion	**l'oignon** (m)	[onioun]
open	**ouvert**	[oovair]
orange (color)	**orange**	[oraunj]
orange (fruit)	**l'orange** (f)	[oraunj]

orchard	**le verger**	[verjeh]
orderly	**le brancardier**	[braunkardieh]
ornament	**le bibelot**	[beebelow]
ostrich	**l'autruche** (f)	[otrush]
out	**dehors**	[duh-or]
oval	**l'ovale** (m)	[ovahl]
over	**au-dessus**	[oh-dessoo]
overcoat	**le manteau**	[mauntoe]
owl	**la chouette**	[shooait]

p

pacifier	**la suce**	[sooss]
pail	**le seau**	[soh]
paintbrush	**le pinceau**	[punnsoh]
painting	**la peinture**	[puntur]
paint pot	**le pot de peinture**	[poh-duh-puntur]
paints	**la boîte à peinture**	[bwat-ah-puntur]
pajamas	**le pyjama**	[peejahmah]
pancake	**la crêpe**	[krehp]
panda	**le panda**	[paundah]
pants	**le pantalon**	[pauntalong]
pantyhose	**le collant**	[kohlaun]
paper	**le papier**	[papeeyeh]
paper chain	**la chaîne de papier**	[shen-duh papeeyeh]
paper cup	**le gobelet en papier**	[gobeleh-aun-papeeyeh]
paper towel	**l'essuie-tout** (m)	[eswi-too]
paramedic	**l'ambulancier** (m)	[ambulaun-sieh]
park	**le parc**	[park]
parking meter	**le parcmètre**	[park-metr]
park keeper	**le gardien de parc**	[gardiun-duh-park]
parrot	**le perroquet**	[pehrokeh]
party	**la fête**	[fet]
party bag	**le sac de fête**	[sak-duh-fet]
party dress	**la robe d'anniversaire**	[rob-danivairsair]
party hat	**le chapeau en papier**	[shapoh-on-papeeyeh]
passport	**le passeport**	[passepor]
pasta	**les pâtes** (f)	[paht]
path	**le chemin**	[shemun]
patient	**le patient**	[pahsaeeyaun]
patrol car	**la voiture de police**	[vwatur-duh-poliss]
pea	**le pois**	[pwa]

peacock	**le paon**	[paun]
pear	**la poire**	[pwar]
pebble	**le galet**	[galeh]
pelican	**le pélican**	[pelikaun]
pencil	**le crayon**	[krayoun]
penguin	**le pingouin**	[pungooun]
people	**les gens** (m)	[jaun]
pepper	**le poivre**	[pwavr]
phone booth	**la cabine téléphonique**	[kabeen-telefonik]
photograph	**la photo**	[foto]
piano	**le piano**	[piano]
pick	**cueillir**	[keyeer]
picnic	**le pique-nique**	[piknik]
picnic table	**la table de pique-nique**	[tabl-duh-piknik]
picture	**le tableau**	[tabloe]
pig	**le cochon**	[koshon]
pigeon	**le pigeon**	[peejon]
piglet	**le petit cochon**	[petee-koshon]
pigpen	**la porcherie**	[porsheree]
pill	**le cachet**	[kasheh]
pillow	**l'oreiller** (m)	[oreyeh]
pilot	**le/la pilote**	[peelot]
pineapple	**l'ananas** (m)	[ahnahnahss]
pink	**rose**	[rohz]
pipe	**le tuyau**	[tueeh-yo]
pirate	**le pirate**	[peerat]
pitcher	**le pichet**	[peesheh]
pizza	**la pizza**	[pidza]
plant	**la plante**	[plaunt]
plaster cast	**le plâtre**	[plahtr]
plate	**l'assiette** (f)	[asseeyet]
platform	**le quai**	[keh]
play	**jouer**	[jooeh]
playing card	**la carte à jouer** (f)	[kart-ah-jooeh]
plow	**la charrue**	[sharoo]
plug (electric)	**la prise de courant**	[preez-duh-koohraun]
plug (washbasin)	**le bouchon**	[booshoun]
plum	**la prune**	[prun]
plumber	**le plombier**	[plombieh]
polar bear	**l'ours polaire** (m)	[oors-pohlair]
police officer	**le policier**	[poleesieh]
pond	**le bassin**	[bassun]
popcorn	**le maïs éclaté**	[ma-ees-ehklateh]
popsicle	**la sucette glacée**	[soosett-glahseh]

porcupine	**le porc-épic**	[pork-ehpik]
poster	**l'affiche** (f)	[afeesh]
potato	**la pomme de terre**	[pom-duh-tair]
potato chips	**les croustilles** (f)	[kroosteey]
pot glove	**la mitaine à four**	[meeten-ah-foor]
pottery maker (man)	**le potier**	[pohtieh]
pottery maker (woman)	**la potière**	[pohtiair]
printer	**l'imprimante** (f)	[imprimaunt]
puffin	**le macareux**	[makareu]
pull	**tirer**	[teereh]
puppet	**la marionnette**	[mareeonett]
purple	**violet**	[veeoleh]
purse	**le sac à main**	[sak-ah-munh]
push	**pousser**	[poosseh]

r

rabbit	**le lapin**	[lapun]
raccoon	**le raton laveur**	[rahton-lahver]
racing car	**la voiture de course**	[vwatur-duh-koors]
radiator	**le radiateur**	[rahdee-yahter]
radio	**la radio**	[rahdioh]
raft	**le radeau**	[radoh]
railroad station	**la gare**	[gar]
rain	**la pluie**	[pluewee]
rainbow	**l'arc-en-ciel** (m)	[ark-aun-siel]
raincoat	**l'imperméable** (m)	[unpermeh-abl]
rake	**le râteau**	[ratoh]
rattle	**le hochet**	[osheh]
read	**lire**	[leer]
receipt	**le reçu**	[ressoo]
receptionist	**le réceptionniste**	[resep-sioneest]
recorder	**la flûte à bec**	[floot-ah-beck]
rectangle	**le rectangle**	[retaungle]
red	**rouge**	[rooj]
reindeer	**le renne**	[rehn]
restaurant	**le restaurant**	[restoraun]
rhinoceros	**le rhinocéros**	[reenoseross]
ribbon	**le ruban**	[roobaun]
rice	**le riz**	[ree]
riding	**l'équitation** (f)	[ekitaseeyoun]
ringmaster	**Monsieur Loyal**	[monssieu-lwahyahl]

river	**la rivière**	[reeviair]
road	**la route**	[root]
robot	**le robot**	[robo]
rock	**le rocher**	[rosheh]
rocket	**la fusée**	[fuzeh]
rocking chair	**la chaise berçante**	[shaiz-bairsaunt]
rocking horse	**le cheval à bascule**	[sherval-ah-baskul]
rockpool	**la mare**	[marr]
roller-coaster	**les montagnes russes** (f)	[montahgn-roos]
roller skates	**les patins à roulette** (m)	[patun-ah-roolett]
rolling pin	**le rouleau à pâtisserie**	[roolo-ah-pateeseree]
roof	**le toit**	[twa]
rooster	**le coq**	[kok]
rope	**la corde**	[kord]
row	**ramer**	[rameh]
rowing	**l'aviron** (m)	[aveeroun]
rug	**le tapis**	[tahpee]
rugby	**le rugby**	[rugby]
ruler	**la règle**	[regl]
run	**courir**	[kooreer]

s

sack	**le sac**	[sak]
sad	**triste**	[treest]
saddle	**la selle**	[sehl]
sail	**la voile**	[vwal]
sailboat	**le voilier**	[vwaleeyeh]
sailing	**la voile**	[vwal]
sailor	**le marin**	[marunh]
salad	**la salade**	[sahlahd]
salt	**le sel**	[sehl]
sand	**le sable**	[sahbl]
sandal	**la sandale**	[saundahl]
sandbox	**le bac à sable**	[bak-ah-sabl]
sandcastle	**le château de sable**	[shatoh-duh-sahbl]
sandwich	**le sandwich**	[sonweej]
Saturday	**samedi**	[samdee]
saucepan	**la casserole**	[kasserol]
saucer	**la soucoupe**	[sookoop]
sausage	**la saucisse**	[sohseess]
scales	**la balance**	[balauns]
scarecrow	**l'épouvantail** (m)	[epoovaun-taye]
scarf	**l'écharpe** (f)	[ehsharp]
school	**l'école** (f)	[ekol]

scientist	le/la scientifique	[siaunteefeek]
scissors	les ciseaux	[seezoh]
scooter	la patinette	[pattinett]
sea	la mer	[mair]
seagull	la mouette	[muwett]
seal	l'otarie (f)	[otaree]
season	la saison	[sayzohn]
seat	le banc	[baun]
seaweed	l'algue (f)	[alg]
secretary	le/la secrétaire	[sekretair]
seed	la graine	[grehn]
seesaw	la bascule	[baskul]
September	septembre	[septaumbr]
seven	sept	[set]
seventeen	dix-sept	[deesset]
shampoo	le shampooing	[shampooun]
shape	la forme	[form]
shark	le requin	[rekun]
shed	la remise	[remeez]
sheep	le mouton	[mooton]
sheepdog	le chien de berger	[shiun-duh-bergeh]
sheet	le drap	[dra]
shelf	l'étagère (f)	[etahjair]
shell	le coquillage	[kokeeyahj]
shirt	la chemise	[shumeez]
shoe	la chaussure	[shossur]
shopping cart	le chariot	[sharioh]
short	court	[koor]
shorts	le short	[short]
shoulder	l'épaule (f)	[epohl]
shovel	la pelle	[pehl]
shower	la douche	[doosh]
shrimp	la crevette	[krevett]
sidewalk	le trottoir	[trotwar]
sing	chanter	[shaunteh]
singer (man)	le chanteur	[shaunter]
singer (woman)	la chanteuse	[shaunteuz]
sink	l'évier (m)	[eveeyeh]
sister	la soeur	[ser]
sit	s'asseoir	[saswar]
six	six	[sees]
sixteen	seize	[sehz]
skateboard	le skateboard	[skateboard]
skiing	le ski	[skee]
skip	sauter à la corde	[sohteh-ah-la-kord]
skirt	la jupe	[joop]
sky	le ciel	[see-el]
sleep	dormir	[dormeer]
sleeping bag	le sac de couchage	[sak-duh-kooshaj]
slide	la glissoire	[gleeswar]
sling	l'écharpe (f)	[esharp]
slipper	la pantoufle	[pontoofl]
slow	lent	[laun]
small	petit	[peutee]
smile	sourire	[sooreer]
smoke	la fumée	[fumeh]
snail	l'escargot (m)	[eskargo]
snake	le serpent	[sehrpaun]
sneaker	la basket	[basket]
snorkel	le tube	[toob]
snow	la neige	[nej]
snow boarding	la planche à neige	[plaunsh-ah-nej]
soap	le savon	[savon]
soccer	le football	[footbal]
sock	la chaussette	[shoset]
soft	doux	[doo]
soil	la terre	[tair]
soldier	le petit soldat	[peutee-soldah]
soup	la soupe	[soop]
spaghetti	les spaghettis (m)	[spagettee]
sparkler	le cierge magique	[sierj-majeek]
sponge	l'éponge (f)	[eponj]
spoon	la cuiller	[kweeyer]
sport	le sport	[spor]
spring	le printemps (m)	[pruntaun]
sprinkler	l'arroseur (m)	[arozer]
square	le carré	[karreh]
squash	le squash	[squash]
stable	l'écurie (f)	[ekuree]
stand	se tenir debout	[suh-teneer-duhboo]
stand in line	faire la queue	[fair-la-keu]
star	l'étoile (f)	[etwal]
starfish	l'étoile de mer (f)	[etwal-duh-mair]
steak	le steak	[stehk]
step	la marche	[marsh]
stethoscope	le stéthoscope	[stetoscope]
sticking plaster	le pansement	[paunsmaun]
stool	le tabouret	[tahbooreh]
store	le magasin	[magazzan]
stove	la cuisinière	[kwiziniair]
straw (drinking)	la paille	[pahye]
straw	la paille	[pahye]
strawberry	la fraise	[frez]
street	la rue	[roo]
stretcher	la civière	[seeviair]
string	la corde	[kord]

stroller	**la poussette**	[poohsett]	tennis	**le tennis**	[tennees]
sucker	**la sucette**	[soossett]	tent	**la tente**	[taunt]
sugar	**le sucre**	[sookr]	thermometer	**le thermomètre**	[termomehtr]
suitcase	**la valise**	[valeez]	thin	**mince**	[muns]
summer	**l'été** (m)	[ehteh]	thirteen	**treize**	[trehz]
sun	**le soleil**	[solay]	three	**trois**	[trwa]
sun cream	**la crème solaire**	[krem-solair]	thumb	**le pouce**	[pouss]
Sunday	**dimanche**	[deemaunsh]	thumb tack	**la punaise**	[punehz]
sunglasses	**les lunettes de soleil** (f)	[loonett-duh-solay]	Thursday	**jeudi**	[jeuhdee]
			ticket	**le billet**	[beeyeh]
sunhat	**le chapeau de soleil**	[shapoh-duh-solay]	ticket booth	**la billetterie**	[beeyehteree]
			tiger	**le tigre**	[teegr]
sunshade	**le parasol**	[parasol]	tightrope walker	**l'équilibriste** (m/f)	[ehkeelee-breest]
supermarket	**le supermarché**	[super-marsheh]	tissue	**le mouchoir en papier**	[mooshwar-aun-papeeyeh]
surf board	**la planche de surf**	[plonsh-duh-surf]			
surfing	**le surf**	[surf]	toad	**le crapaud**	[krapoh]
swan	**le cygne**	[seehgn]	toast	**le pain grillé**	[pun-greeyeh]
sweater	**le chandail**	[shaunday]	toaster	**le grille-pain**	[greeye-pun]
swim	**nager**	[najeh]	toboggan	**le toboggan**	[tobogaun]
swimming	**la natation**	[nataseeoun]	toe	**le doigt de pied**	[dwa-duh-pee-eh]
swimming pool	**la piscine**	[peehseen]			
swimsuit	**le maillot de bain**	[myoh-duh-baun]	toilet	**les toilettes** (f)	[twalett]
			tomato	**la tomate**	[tomatt]
swing	**la balançoire**	[balaunswar]	tongue	**la langue**	[laung]
switch	**l'interrupteur** (m)	[untairupter]	tool set	**la boîte à outils**	[bwat-ah-ootee]
			toothbrush	**la brosse à dents**	[bros-ah-daun]
t					
table	**la table**	[tahbl]	toothpaste	**le dentifrice**	[dauntee-freess]
tablecloth	**la nappe**	[nap]			
table tennis	**le tennis de table**	[tennees-duh-tahbl]	top hat	**le chapeau haut de forme**	[shapoh-oh-duh-form]
tadpole	**le têtard**	[tehtar]	toucan	**le toucan**	[toucaun]
tank	**l'aquarium** (m)	[akwariom]	towel	**la serviette**	[serviett]
tanker	**le camion-citerne**	[kameeon-seetairn]	towel rail	**le porte-serviettes**	[port-serviett]
			town	**la ville**	[veel]
tea	**le thé**	[tay]	tow truck	**la dépanneuse**	[daypaneuz]
teacher	**la maîtresse**	[mehtress]	toy	**le jouet**	[jweh]
teapot	**la théière**	[tayair]	toybox	**la boîte à jouets**	[bwat-ah-jweh]
teddy bear	**l'ours en peluche** (m)	[oors-en-peloosh]	toy store	**le magasin de jouets**	[magazun-duh-jweh]
teeth	**les dents** (f)	[daun]	track	**le rail**	[rahy]
telephone	**le téléphone**	[telefon]	tractor	**le tracteur**	[trakter]
television	**la télévision**	[teleh-veezeeong]	traffic cone	**le cône**	[kohn]
			trailer	**la caravane**	[karavan]
television host (man)	**le présentateur**	[prezauntater]	train	**le train**	[trun]
			train engineer	**le conducteur**	[kondukter]
television host (woman)	**la présentatrice**	[prezaunta-treez]	trampoline	**le trampoline**	[trampoleen]
			trash can	**la boîte à ordures**	[bwat-ah-ordewr]
ten	**dix**	[dees]			

tray	**le plateau**	[platoh]
tree	**l'arbre** (m)	[arbr]
triangle	**le triangle**	[treeaungle]
tricycle	**le tricycle**	[treeseekl]
trough	**l'abreuvoir** (m)	[abrevooar]
trowel	**le transplantoir**	[traunsplaun-twar]
truck	**le camion**	[kameeoun]
truck driver	**le camionneur**	[kameey oneur]
trumpet	**la trompette**	[trompett]
trunk (car)	**le coffre**	[kofr]
T-shirt	**le T-shirt**	[tee-shirt]
Tuesday	**mardi**	[mardee]
tummy	**le ventre**	[vauntr]
tunnel	**le tunnel**	[toonail]
turkey	**la dinde**	[dund]
turtle	**la tortue**	[tortu]
tweezers	**la pince à épiler**	[puns-ah-epeeleh]
twelve	**douze**	[dooz]
twenty	**vingt**	[vun]
twig	**la brindille**	[brundeehy]
two	**deux**	[duh]

U

umbrella	**le parapluie**	[pahrah-pluhwee]
uncle	**l'oncle** (m)	[onk-l]
under	**en dessous**	[aun-dessoo]
underpants	**le caleçon**	[kalessoun]
undershirt	**le tricot**	[treeko]
up	**haut**	[oh]

V

vacuum cleaner	**l'aspirateur** (m)	[aspeerater]
van	**la camionnette**	[kameeyonett]
vase	**le vase**	[vahz]
vegetable	**le légume**	[legewm]
vest	**le gilet de costume**	[jeeleh-duh-kostum]
video recorder	**le magnétoscope**	[maneeayto-scope]
violin	**le violon**	[veeyoloun]

W

wading pool	**la pataugeuse**	[patojeuz]
wagon	**la remorque**	[remork]
waist	**la taille**	[thai]
waiter	**le serveur**	[sairver]
waitress	**la serveuse**	[sairveuz]

walk	**marcher**	[marsheh]
walking frame	**le déambulateur**	[dayaum-boolater]
walking stick	**la canne**	[kan]
wall	**le mur**	[mur]
wardrobe	**l'armoire** (f)	[ar-mwar]
wash	**laver**	[laveh]
washbasin	**le lavabo**	[lahvahboh]
washcloth	**le gant de toilette**	[gaun-duh-twalett]
washing machine	**la machine à laver**	[masheen-ah-laveh]
wasp	**la guêpe**	[ghep]
wastebasket	**la corbeille à papier**	[korbay-ahpapeeyeh]
watch	**la montre**	[montr]
water	**l'eau** (f)	[oh]
waterfall	**la chute d'eau**	[shoot-doh]
watering can	**l'arrosoir** (m)	[arozwar]
watermelon	**la pastèque**	[pasteck]
water-skiing	**le ski nautique**	[skee-noteek]
waterslide	**le toboggan**	[tobogaun]
wave	**la vague**	[vag]
weather	**le temps**	[taum]
Wednesday	**mercredi**	[mairkredee]
week	**la semaine**	[suhmen]
weight lifting	**les haltères** (m)	[altair]
wet	**mouillé**	[mooyeh]
wetsuit	**la combinaison**	[kombeen-ehzon]
whale	**la baleine**	[bahlehn]
wheat	**le blé**	[bleh]
wheel	**la roue**	[roo]
wheelbarrow	**la brouette**	[broowett]
wheelchair	**le fauteuil roulant**	[foteuy-roolaun]
whistle	**le sifflet**	[seeflay]
white	**blanc**	[blaun]
whiteboard	**le tableau**	[tabloh]
wind	**le vent**	[vaun]
windmill	**le moulin**	[moolun]
window	**la fenêtre**	[fenaitr]
window cleaner	**le laveur de carreaux**	[laver-duh-karo]
windsurfing	**la planche à voile**	[plaunsh-ah-vwal]
wing	**l'aile** (f)	[el]
winter	**l'hiver** (m)	[eevair]
witch	**la sorcière**	[sorsiair]
wizard	**le sorcier**	[sorsieh]
wolf	**le loup**	[loo]
woman	**la femme**	[fam]